D1123313

21st
Century
Skills Library

COOL ARTS CAREERS

DANCER

KATIE MARSICO

CHERRY
LAKE
Publishing

Published in the United States of America by
Cherry Lake Publishing, Ann Arbor, Michigan
www.cherrylakepublishing.com

Content Adviser
Lorena Free, Co-Director, Lynette's School of Dance, Park Ridge, Illinois

Photo Credits
Cover and page 1, ©Yuri Arcurs/Shutterstock, Inc.; page 4, ©Jackq/Dreamstime.com; page 7, ©iStockphoto.com/antares71; page 8, ©Sean Nel/Shutterstock, Inc.; page 9, ©iStockphoto.com/RamiKatzav; page 10, ©iStockphoto.com/Gewitterkind; page 13, ©iStockphoto.com/mcpix; pages 15, 21, 24, and 28, ©ASSOCIATED PRESS; page 16, ©Sokolovsky/Dreamstime.com; page 18, ©iStockphoto.com/CEFutcher; page 19, ©Mike Goldwater/Alamy; page 23, ©iStockphoto.com/craftvision; page 26, ©Rebecca Erol/Alamy

Library of Congress Cataloging-in-Publication Data
Marsico, Katie, 1980–
  Dancer/by Katie Marsico.
    p. cm.—(Cool arts careers)
  Includes index.
  ISBN-13: 978-1-61080-130-0 (lib. bdg.)
  ISBN-10: 1-61080-130-X (lib. bdg.)
  1. Dance. I. Title. II. Series.
  GV1597.M37 2011
  792.8—dc22   2011000374

Cherry Lake Publishing would like to acknowledge
the work of The Partnership for 21st Century Skills.
Please visit *www.21stcenturyskills.org* for more information.

Printed in the United States of America
Corporate Graphics Inc.
July 2011
CLFA09

TABLE OF CONTENTS

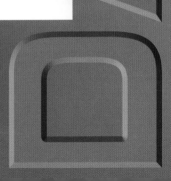

CHAPTER ONE
USING MOVEMENT TO SHARE A STORY

E mma could not take her eyes off the stage. She had never been to a ballet before. She was attending

A ballerina performs the role of Odile as she dances with the prince in Swan Lake.

a **production** of *Swan Lake* with her aunt and uncle. It is the story of a princess who is turned into a swan by an evil magician.

During the performance, people in the audience whispered about how graceful the dancers were and how beautiful the music was. Emma was even more amazed by the way the performers onstage told the swan princess's tale without saying a word. Instead, they used movement to show their characters' feelings and personalities.

Emma stood up and clapped as the curtain fell at the end of the ballet. She had always known that dancing was fun and good exercise. Now she realized that it was also a creative way to share stories.

There are many other types of dance in addition to ballet. Hip-hop, jazz, modern, folk, and tap are some popular performance styles. Professional dancers rely on different **techniques** and settings to tell stories or share ideas with the audience. Some perform in operas and musical theater productions. Others dance in films, television shows, commercials, and music videos.

"Movement and dance are some of the most **primal**, basic things human beings do," explains Louise Reichlin. She is the managing and artistic director of Los Angeles **Choreographers** & Dancers, in California. This non-profit organization offers classes that let people of all ages and backgrounds explore dance. Reichlin has been a professional dancer for 51 years. She has learned the powerful effect that dance can have on an audience.

"In many ways, movement expresses more than words and music do," she says. "Babies communicate with movement before they can even speak. I guess I see great importance in movement because it involves [natural] and unconscious behavior that is also very honest."

LIFE & CAREER SKILLS

You can start preparing for a career as a dancer while you're still in grade school. Louise Reichlin recommends taking as many dance and movement classes as possible. She adds that kids who are interested in becoming dancers can also practice in their own homes.

"It's important to listen to all different kinds of music," Reichlin advises. "And dance whenever you can. For example, dance in your living room when there's music playing on the television or the radio!" What else might help you along the path to a career as a professional dancer?

There are many kinds of dance to learn.

Moving your body to tell a story or communicate a message is not as easy as you may think! Professional dancers need talent and **stamina**. They also need to understand music, **rhythm**, and technique. They spend a lot of time moving their bodies during **auditions**, **rehearsals**, and performances. Do you want to learn what your average day might be like if you end up choosing this career?

Dancers practice long hours to perfect their movements.

Flamenco dancers create a
rhythm with their feet and hands.

CHAPTER TWO

A DAY IN A DANCER'S SHOES

Maria woke up as soon as she heard the alarm clock ring. She had a busy day ahead of her. But she was

It is important for a dancer to keep track of rehearsals, auditions, and other appointments.

used to the life of a professional dancer. Maria ate a healthy breakfast and then packed her tap shoes and water bottle in a duffel bag. She put on exercise pants, a tank top, thin socks, and sneakers.

Before leaving the house, Maria reviewed her schedule one last time. She had tap class at the dance **studio** in the morning. After that, she had four hours of rehearsal with her dance **company**. Later in the afternoon, Maria was auditioning for a small part in a film that needed tap dancers. Finally, she had to head back to the dance studio to help teach a tap class for children.

Maria enjoyed showing other people how to dance. She was also happy to earn a little extra money. Her busy schedule kept her on her toes!

Not everyone with a dance career has the same schedule as Maria. Yet almost all professional dancers are just as busy. Dancers' daily activities depend on what kinds of jobs they have. For example, someone who is trying to find work might attend more auditions than someone who already has a long-term job. In addition, different companies require different time commitments for rehearsals and performances.

Dancers perform everywhere from small studios to huge auditoriums. Some professional dancers move to New York City because they hope to perform on **Broadway**. Others head to Los Angeles, where they try to find jobs in films and television shows.

Professional dancers devote much of their time to practicing. Attending dance classes is one way to do this. Louise Reichlin recommends that dancers try to fit in at least two classes each day.

"A huge part of a dancer's schedule is training," she explains. "Without attending classes and practicing, your body and mind will never get to a place where your body does what your mind wants it to." Reichlin also notes that dance classes help build stamina.

Daily rehearsals can last between 3 and 8 hours. Some dancers have an average of one to six performances a day. Meanwhile, they have to stay warmed up for auditions. Some also have to stay alert during side jobs that they work for extra money. No matter how busy they are, they must find time to eat healthy meals and get plenty of sleep. Dancers depend on healthy bodies to learn, practice, and perform.

Dancers also need the right shoes and clothes. Dance instructors and costume designers help decide what the performers wear. For instance, ballet dancers often need special slippers, tights, and leotards for class. Ballet teachers prefer these clothes because they reveal more about a student's **form** than loose-fitting outfits do. It is important for ballet dancers to be aware of how they are posing their bodies.

On the other hand, tap instructors often ask students to dress in exercise pants, T-shirts, and tap shoes. They are less concerned about a person's form than ballet teachers are.

Instead, tap instructors focus on how students use movement and the tapping sound of their shoes to express rhythm.

Teachers are not the only ones who decide what dancers wear. Costume designers choose outfits for dancers in musicals, films, and other productions. They pick clothes and makeup that reflect the production's theme. They also make sure the costumes allow dancers to perform their moves safely and comfortably.

Can you imagine being fitted for a costume as you prepare to dance in front of thousands of people? How can you make this dream a reality? Get ready to find out!

LIFE & CAREER SKILLS

Being a successful dancer takes more than a few fancy foot moves. Professional dancers need excellent communication skills. They also need the ability to think quickly under pressure. Dancers must be able to follow directions from teachers and choreographers. Knowing how to read music and count musical beats helps them do this.

Such knowledge also allows dancers to perform without much preparation. Professionals can't panic when they face last-minute changes to a routine. Successful dancers can ask choreographers clear questions and adjust to new situations.

These dancers are being fitted for tutus in preparation for a performance of The Nutcracker.

CHAPTER THREE
BECOMING A PROFESSIONAL DANCER

Tim tried to relax as he walked into the local performing arts center. He had practiced his routine, but it was hard

By practicing in front of a mirror, a dancer can see what movements need correcting or adjusting.

not to be nervous. It was his first professional audition. Tim had been taking dance and movement classes since he was 10 years old. Seven years later, he knew he wanted a career in modern dance.

His older sister, Sara, also planned to become a professional dancer. She started studying ballet when she was 5 years old. Like Tim, she took summer classes at a nearby academy that was owned by a famous dance company. The courses they had taken were for students between the ages of 13 and 18. The academy also offered classes for older dancers who wanted to train with the company full-time. Sara decided that this was the right step for her when she graduated from high school.

Tim was happy for his sister, but he wanted to go to college. He knew a college degree wasn't required to become a professional dancer. But he wanted to study art and literature along with music and dance.

Like Tim and Sara, people who want to dance professionally have a few options. Many of these people start dancing at very young ages. Louise Reichlin got her start as a child. "I basically began dancing as soon as I was walking," she says. "I started lessons when I was 5, though they mainly involved improvisational and modern styles. I moved on to ballet in high school."

Teenagers who are serious about dance careers often try to enroll in preprofessional programs offered by dance companies and academies. They take these classes during the summer or after school. Preprofessional training builds new skills in a particular style of dance. It is also an opportunity to meet choreographers and other business contacts.

Several colleges and universities allow students to earn their bachelor's and master's degrees in dance. Many dance students also take classes in history, literature, art, and music. These subjects can add to their understanding of certain productions.

College students hoping to earn a degree in dance often take courses in a wide variety of subjects, including history and literature.

College dance students work on the choreography for an upcoming performance.

Not all professional dancers have college degrees, though. Young dancers may instead decide to train at a school that is owned and operated by a dance company. These dancers are often interested in studying with certain choreographers. Many have already participated in a company's preprofessional summer programs when they enroll as full-time students.

LEARNING & INNOVATION SKILLS

Dancers have an easier time finding work as they gain more professional experience and become known. Some take on other roles in their companies. For example, some become ballet mistresses and masters, and are responsible for instructing dancers and overseeing rehearsals. In addition, professional dancers may eventually decide to develop careers in choreography or artistic direction. Other dancers look for teaching jobs at schools and studios. Many even offer private lessons out of their homes.

Most dancers realize early on that auditions will make up a large part of their career. It is common for dancers to begin

A dancer rehearses Cambodian classical dance at the Phnom Penh School of Fine Arts.

auditioning for professional work between the ages of 17 and 18. Yet it is also important to remember that even the most talented performers don't get every job they want.

Reichlin encourages dancers not to give up if they don't receive offers as soon as they start auditioning. "Try not to get too personal about rejection," she advises. "It is one of the most difficult parts of being a dancer."

Dancers don't receive a job offer after every audition. This means they need to be flexible and creative in order to earn a steady salary. Dancing jobs are often short-term. They do not always pay well. A large number of dancers must take on extra jobs that are not related to dancing. Professional dancers earn anywhere from $7.28 to $27.26 an hour. The average hourly wage in 2008 was $12.22. How much dancers are paid depends on their experience and who they work for. Some dancers belong to **unions** that guarantee benefits and a minimum wage.

Are you starting to see how a dance career requires determination and effort? Working as a dancer is challenging, but it can also be very rewarding.

Many dancers also teach dance classes.

CHAPTER FOUR
LOOKING TOWARD THE FUTURE

Ella could barely contain her excitement. She had received a phone call from a choreographer about last week's

Competition for spots in professional dance companies can be fierce.

audition. The choreographer was producing an Irish dance show and wanted to hire her! Ella had spent years training to be an Irish dancer, but it still wasn't easy to find work.

One of Ella's teachers said that it had been hard to find work when she began dancing in the 1990s. She told Ella that the competition for jobs had gotten tougher since then. She also believed that things would probably remain tough in the future. Ella knew that her teacher was right. She had seen several dance companies cut performances or even close because of money troubles.

In addition, most of the productions that Ella had danced in only needed her for short periods of time. She auditioned often. But the performers she was competing against were also talented and dedicated. As a result, Ella was thrilled whenever she received a job offer. Ella knew that training and hard work alone didn't guarantee regular job opportunities. She understood that she would have to keep working hard to develop a successful career.

Professional dancers face stiff competition for jobs. It is also difficult for dancers to find jobs that last longer than a few months at a time. This means that dancers must look for new jobs more often than people in most other careers.

In addition, cuts to public and private funding could make it difficult for smaller dance companies and performance groups to operate. This also can limit the number of available dance jobs.

Lastly, some dancers fear that the use of computers and new technology will reduce the value of dancing as a communication tool. But professionals such as Louise Reichlin are able to look past these concerns. Reichlin encourages future performers to be both hopeful and realistic about the future.

"You can't learn to dance sitting in front of a computer," she says. "Nor do you have to be part of a huge, multimillion-dollar company to achieve success or make a difference."

Audience members watch as two ballet dancers take their bows.

No matter how technology and the economy change, Americans will likely continue to be entertained and impressed by professional dancers well into the future.

Can you picture yourself using your feet to communicate a message or share a story? Maybe one day it will be you who bows in front of a cheering audience as the curtain falls!

21ST CENTURY CONTENT

How has new technology helped professional dancers? New software allows dancers to create and view choreography on their computers. Handheld devices such as MP3 players give them easy access to a variety of music and dance videos. Finally, dance performances and competitions that are broadcast on television and the Internet have become very popular in the past few years.

Mikhail Baryshnikov dances with ballerina Yvonne Borree.

SOME FAMOUS DANCERS

Fred Astaire (1899–1987) enjoyed fame and popularity as an actor and dancer in American film and stage productions. He is perhaps best known for his skill in tap and ballroom dance. Astaire was born in Omaha, Nebraska. He often danced alongside another talented performer named Ginger Rogers. He made a total of 31 musical films and is thought of as one of the greatest dancers in movie history.

Josephine Baker (1906–1975) was an African American entertainer and activist. She was widely known as a jazz singer and dancer in the United States and France. She was born in Saint Louis, Missouri, though she eventually moved to France. Before her fame, she worked as a chorus dancer in variety shows. She rose above racial discrimination in the United States and France to develop a successful performance career. She impressed audiences with her unique singing and expressive jazz moves.

Mikhail Baryshnikov (1948–) was born and raised in Russia, where he spent several years performing professional ballet. He moved to the United States and began working with the American Ballet Theatre (ABT) in 1974. He became ABT's artistic director in 1980. Since then, he has worked on projects that aim to inspire young dancers and celebrate contemporary ballet. He has also appeared in numerous films and television shows. In 2005, he established New York City's Baryshnikov Arts Center.

Martha Graham (1894–1991) is considered one of the most important shapers of modern dance. She was born in Pittsburgh, Pennsylvania, but eventually traveled the world. Her movements defined modern dance by showing a wide range of human emotions. She spent more than 70 years working as a dancer and choreographer. She even made her mark at the White House in Washington, D.C. She was the first professional dancer to perform there for the president!

GLOSSARY

auditions (aw-DIH-shuhnz) performances that dancers give in the hopes of winning a part in a production

Broadway (BRAWD-way) a street in New York City that is the center of a world-famous theater district

choreographers (kor-ee-AH-graf-uhrz) people who plan or create dances

company (KUHM-puh-nee) an organization of dancers or other performers

form (FORM) the way a dancer positions his or her body in keeping with certain performance techniques

primal (PRYE-muhl) primitive

production (pruh-DUHK-shuhn) a play, dance performance, or any other show that is presented to an audience

rehearsals (ri-HUHR-suhlz) practice sessions that occur before a performance

rhythm (RIH-thuhm) the pattern of beats that sets the pace in a piece of music

stamina (STAH-muh-nuh) lasting strength and energy

studio (STU-dee-oh) space for teaching and practicing dance

techniques (tek-NEEKS) ways of doing something to create different styles of dance

unions (YOON-yuhnz) organizations of employees that bargain with employers for benefits and pay requirements

FOR MORE INFORMATION

BOOKS

Gladstone, Valerie, and José Ivey (photographer). *A Young Dancer: The Life of an Ailey Student.* New York: Henry Holt, 2009.

Nathan, Amy. *Meet the Dancers: From Ballet, Broadway, and Beyond.* New York: Henry Holt, 2008.

Nelson, Marilyn, and Susan Kuklin (photographer). *Beautiful Ballerina.* New York: Scholastic Press, 2009.

WEB SITES

Los Angeles Choreographers & Dancers
www.lachoreographersanddancers.org
LAChoreographersAndDancers.org/index.html
Visit this Web page for a closer look at Louise Reichlin's organization and career.

United States Department of Labor: Bureau of Labor Statistics—Dancer
www.bls.gov/k12/sports01.htm
Read an overview of professional dance, including specific job descriptions and information on training and income.

INDEX

ABOUT THE AUTHOR

Katie Marsico has written more than 80 books for young readers. She dedicates this book to her own budding dancer, Maria.